In & Out of Love

POETIC AFFIRMATIONS

MARION D. INGRAM

Also by Marion Ingram

Uncensored Thoughts: The Things We Never Say
The State of America

For Gerald,
Lillian,
&
The late Mary B. Cooper

In & Out of Love

POETIC AFFIRMATIONS

Editors: Marcus Dillon and Tyrone Dumas

Illustration Page 39 © 2014 Gloria Marconi

Cover Design and Photo © 2014 Paulo Salud
Printed in the United States of America

mrmarion@mail.com
www.mrmarion.com
For additional copies of this book
go to Amazon.com

ISBN: 978-1502588036

Table of Contents

Table of Contents

Introduction

Love: there are not many words that come with more compactness than this one. Not many words can make someone's day livelier while instantaneously causing someone else great melancholy. Our tender human hearts magnetically connect to unsuspecting embrace daringly. They say Love, if unrequited, still triggers very strong emotional feelings and reactions but for very different reasons. Love has started and ended wars—this can be seen many times throughout history. I was always told that it is the glue that holds the world together.

Through *In and Out of Love: Poetic Affirmations*, I strive to unveil and display the very common emotions most associated with love: It is a rigorous task to maintain and manage such feelings. These poems reflect true heartfelt encounters of the body, mind and soul. Whether you are currently experiencing the paradise and harmony of new exciting love; dealing with the melancholy and pain of failing love, these poems provide wisdom and appealing food for thought. These poems describe some of the most passionate tales of love from my heart to yours.

Marion D. Ingram

No Time for Love

Those who have love seem so fulfilled
with endless bliss:
A solid relationship is what they
develop
Hand to hand,
Wrist to wrist,
Those who seek forever never
settle down,
Becoming a possession is the fear to
dreams yet found.

Short term love becomes a
consistent cycle trend;
Seekers dedicated to passion embrace their loneliness within.

The battle of omnipotent righteousness rebuts their sinister fate;

Natural talent always succeeds,
Natural drive always creates,

No time for love.
No time to debate.

A Time for Love

Introducing my family to you
Breaking plans to be with you
Finding time to call you
Distracted with thoughts of you
Hearing love songs reminding me of you
Calling out sick to spend time with you
Working out more to look good for you
Saving money to buy for you
Sacrificing for you
Compromising for you
Wanting to see you
Wanting to show you
Wanting to know you
Wanting to grow with you
I found someone I could make time to love

Human Doormat

*Dedicated to those in emotionally, physically and
verbally abusive relationships*

I let you walk all over me,
Talk all over me,
Circle chalk all over me,
Like a victim lying dead.

I allow you to abuse me,
Use me,
Bring the blues to me,
Like a hostage unfed.

I let you disrespect me,
Reject me,
Affect me,
Like a fool mislead.

I accepted your ego,
Your libido,
Erupting volcano,
Still my legs stayed spread

People see you bash me,
Lash me,
Trash me,
Bring pain to my head.

Every time I leave you,
I grieve you,
Need you,
Go back to what I dread.

Even when your plight I recognize,
I still justify;
Physically hospitalized,
Emotionally hypnotized,
Never testify.

Damn I should have fled

Still when you walk bye
I get butterflies
With black eyes;
Dehumanized thread.

Even when you cheated, I turned and looked the other way;
When you lie I pretend to believe the words you say;
When you walked out I let you back the next day.
And when you return,
On the floor,
By my door,
I will lay.

Human doormat.

Then Came You

I had given up on true love
Unfulfilled by many
Impressed by very few

I placed my heart on pause
Then came you

Out of nowhere you appear
Erased all my deepest fears
Made me feel brand new

They say life is better with someone to share it with
Now I know it's true

They say don't go looking for love
Good love will find you

Life is so much better now
Nothing seems to get me down
I found my perfect Boo

Your presence makes me shiver
In all ways you deliver
The picture gets no bigger

Love couldn't remember

Then came you

Lonely Heart

Absorbing the happiness around you
Wishing someone could make you smile

Walking on sidewalks made of rose thorns
Love has not been around in awhile

Would love to express how you truly feel
But choose to live in denial

Rivers once flowing with love
Now streams of banal

One night stands replacing romantic affairs
No substance, no morale

Warm bar seats and intoxicated tongues
Turning streams to canals

Powdered nostrils and cannabis seeds replacing
Affection and good rationale

You pacify reality
Lose spirituality
No more practicality
Cause your own brutality
The reality
Of
A
Lonely
Heart

You and I

The perfect love
Complimenting each other's passion and goals sincerely true

The combination of trust and faith
No matter what we go through

Always building dreams
Searching for something new

Wanting only the best for each other
In all we pursue

Never let small things hold us back
We got big things to look forward to

Disciplined and grounded
Got loves perfect view

Always got the answer
Always gets the clue

The best thing in my world
Is the life I spend with you

You and I

Karma

Be careful of the things you do
For it surely will come back to you
Watch all the things you say
It will be repeated someday
Be careful of the games you play
You'll get played the same way
Watch the bed you make
It can be the bed you may lay

Be careful of the bridges you burn
You may need to walk that pathway

Watch the hands that you bite
They may feed you one day

Watch the hearts you break
Karma will make you pay

Dedication

To your lips
Your soul
Your body
I'll commit

To your heart
Your love
Your spirit
I'll submit

Not one day
One hour
One second
I'll forget

Not any failure
Hardship
Trials
Will make me quit

No past
No present
No future
Will I fail to admit

Honesty
Commitment
Trust
Loyalty
I'll never omit

The Relapse of a Broken Heart

Thought I had given you up
Like an old habit I used to know

Thought you were someone in my past
That proved we couldn't grow

Thought I had moved on with my life
With no more emotions to show

Thought you were out of my dreams
Good riddance overflow

Thought you already reaped what you sow
Couldn't get more low

Somehow I'm back to where I used to be
Enjoying your company
No longer free
Lost my dignity

Entertaining what's wrong for me

Addictively

The Answer is You

Like a good fortune, you bring good news
Like a love song, you sing no blues

Like a socket outlet, you lite my fuse
Like a winner, you never lose

Like a church offering,
You pay my dues

Like sightseeing in an ocean,
You're my favorite cruise

Like the best choice,
It's you I choose

Like a drunk needs whiskey,
You're my booze

Whenever you're around
I could never refuse

The Answer is You!

Fools In Love

Some people give all they have
And get nothing in return

Some endure so much pain
Still lessons go unlearned

Some people get sucked dry
And never say goodbye

Some people see a bad haiku
And still remain true

Some keep forgiving, waiting for change

Old dogs don't pick up new tricks

Old tricks aren't so strange

Some people rely on others for personal validation
Some emancipate in love and change their situation

Some lose themselves for the love of another
Some seek spiritual grounds to help them recover

Some people put their children in harm
Just to please a lover

Some put their dreams on hold
Just to keep a brother

Some think it's the best they can do
And settle for less

A fool in love
                    Always second best

Forgive Me

For all wrong choices I made
For all the prices you paid

For all the lies I told
For all the weight you hold

For all the boundaries I've crossed
For all the trust I've lost

For all the tears you've cried
For the lack of pride

For all the times I didn't call
For the final straw

For all the deceit I displayed
For being afraid

For all the wrong I've done
You're still the one

I'll be all that you need
If you forgive me

12 Months of Love

In January I start looking for love cold months ahead and
then naturally I'm ready to settle down

February brings cold to the air
And the warmth of love needs to be found

Before the groundhog sees its shadow
March conveys an enjoyable feeling of spring

When April brings showers
The finger gets a ring

In May we're still happy
Fulfilled with sturdy firm trust

June arrives quickly
With challenges of summer lust

In July we survived temptations
Still committed and true

In August things begin to change
We don't do the things we used to do

In September just like the leaves begin to fade
Soul searching comes aboard to see decisions get made

In the month of the Libra October tries to balance things out.
The feelings are fragile; the heart has doubt

November comes with holiday cheer abundantly vast
Great memories of months before now memories of the past

December catches amnesia because the love didn't last

The twelve months of love needs a whole new cast

26

Love Warrior

I'll crawl through the barb wire
Drag my chin through painful dust

I'll run through grenades and bullets
Take a wound if I must

I'll go reluctantly into battle
Watch my steel turn to rust

I'll fight without fear
Just to win your trust

I'll be a knight in stainless armor
To capture all your lust

I'll let action show my words
When words aren't enough

I'll be there to dry your tears
When your heart has been crushed

To Someone Else

Your personality
Congeniality

To Someone Else

Your happiness
Your success

To Someone Else

Your dedication
Your motivation

To Someone Else

Your dreams
Your themes
Extremes

To Someone Else

Your commitment
Your judgment
Intelligence

To Someone Else

Your beautiful eyes
Sweet Brown thighs
No surprise

You belong to someone else

Moving On

Getting over a breakup is no easy task;
While rebounds comes first, feelings go last

Losing someone you love hurts unexplainably
The loss of appetite
Depression
Anxiety

The happy world you became accustomed to
Is now a world that doesn't exist
Thoughts become filled with sudden somber
Pain suddenly covers your wrist
Every song you hear about love
Reminds you of the love you miss

It's time you find the new you
Rediscover true happiness

Eventually you will rise again
Dream again
Hope again
Smile again
Love again

But first you have to move on

I Love You

I wasn't smoking
I wasn't drinking

I wasn't joking
I wasn't playing

I was hoping
I was conveying

I meant every word I was saying
When I said I love you

I wasn't dreaming
I wasn't scheming

I was awake
I wasn't sleeping

I meant every word I was speaking
When you heard me say I love you

I wasn't lying
I wasn't dying

I was typing
I was Skyping

I meant every word I was writing
When I wrote: I LOVE YOU

Co-dependent

I need your affection
Your will
Your drive

I need your vision
Your decisions
Your comfort
Your strive

I need your wisdom
Your hugs
Your smile
Your vibe

I need your touch
Your love
Your existence

To stay alive

Vow Renewal

I promise to show more concern
Be more in touch with time spent with you

I promise to give more of myself
Be more honest and true

I promise to make you feel loved and appreciated
Be more consistent in your view

I promise to be there more mentally

Physically
Financially
Parentally
Consistently
Fundamentally

If you say I do again

The Unscrupulous Journey of a Cheating Heart

I never thought we'd come to this day
While the cat was gone the mouse did play

Phone starts to ring; into the bathroom you go
Taking private calls and speaking very low

Something is funny and there's no debate
Sudden meetings after work; coming home late

Your time spent on Facebook has gotten unusually long
Your status on Twitter said something is going wrong

I'm just being insecure, that's the words you now say
However, you didn't remember my last birthday

My mom was out shopping and guess who she saw
You holding my hand only I was a bit more tall

So as she approached to say "how are you doing?"
She realized it was someone else that you were wooing

When I got the message I was in great disbelief
Denial of the truth spared the throbbing grief

So while you were asleep your phone became my prey
Your incoming texts gave me spot-on dismay

The discovery of you cheating was the least of my shock
The person of your affair put my heart on lock

My best friend, how could you dare?
Now I'm losing two people for whom I truly did care
Foolish of me: I should have seen all the signs
The ravenous eye contact
The extended goodbyes

You fulfilled all my needs thought I was better than the rest
Silly of me, naively second best

They say deceit works best in the darkest of night
But the truth gets and comes to the light

What doesn't come out in the wash eventually comes out in the
rinse. Grandma's old saying abruptly makes sense

It's always sad to find a love being untrue
If it happened to me, it can happen to you

Lying connects to cheating as cheaters will steal
When your heart is at stake, its true pain you will feel

If intuition decides to speak, believe what it will say
Even a broken clock is right twice a day

My First Love

Even as the years have passed by I can still remember
that day.
Never knew love ever existed until you brought it
my way

It was the simple things you did that made me fall so
very deep

The tone in your voice
Your kiss so sweet

You were the perfect midnight breeze
The warmest of summer sun

My tender young heart was helplessly stung

It was sensational moments of my life that can't ever
be replaced

The passionate fire
The moments of embrace

Even to this day I still see your face

My first love will never be erased

The Last Straw

There are some things you forgive even while you don't forget
Some excuses that work while you hate to admit

There is someone to blame for every problem that arises
Some love at stake when you discover piles of lies

There are challenges that occur when one puts down their guard
Some decisions to be made when your heart has been scarred

There are consequences that derive for every action unjust
Some victim to suffer when desire tampers lust

There are lessons to be learned when you give a second chance
Some commit to their promise; some fail true romance

There are changes to be made when you end a dream come true
Some love last a lifetime; some never do

There are reasons you want to stay when you have given love
your all

Some reasons never win once you've had your last straw

What Would You Compromise For Love?

Would you disregard a person's weight if they weren't very in shape?
Would you give someone your heart if they couldn't mentally relate?

Would you marry someone that didn't have a college degree?
Would you commit to someone with an STD?

Would you truly love someone who couldn't spell?
Would you fall in love with someone who lives in jail?

Would you give yourself to someone that was possibly gay?
Would you take whatever came your way?

Would you love someone that was short on cash?
Could you commit to someone who smoked a lot of hash?

Would you marry someone who drank too much rum?
Would you settle for someone who didn't make you come
To the promise land

Would you fall in love with someone who couldn't walk?
That couldn't talk?

Would you stay with someone your family didn't approve?
Someone whose job made them move?
How about someone whom had children with another?
Could you tolerate baby mothers?

Would you stay with someone who had different religious views?
No values?

Would you break a heart for beauty over wealth?
Do you need a partner in good health?

Would you give your love to someone who was many years younger?
Does your perfect love have a perfect number?

Would you share your entire life with someone with no
sense of humor?
Had deadly tumors
Cancer
AIDS
Diabetes
Parkinson's disease
Heart disease
Speech impediments
Unattractive
One leg
One arm
No hair
In a wheel chair
Blind
Broke
Uses coke

What would you compromise for love?

When Love Goes Astray

When there's no understanding
It may be time to walk away

When loves gets too demanding
Why on earth you choose to stay

When emotions start fading
Maybe expiration has reached its day

There's no turning back when love goes astray

When the warm hands that used to touch you feel cold
and hard like steel

When moments of sensuality have lost their thrill

When the bed you share has no romance in sight
When good love may have had its last night

When it feels like you're the only one still trying to fight
When acts of denial can't do what's right

When the price of love is high to pay
When the hardest part of having love is watching it go astray

Crazy For Your Love

Just to keep you hanging around there isn't much I wouldn't do
I'd take a flight from NY to LA just to spend an hour with you

Just to make you smile I'd work my fingers to the bone
Sell my car for extra cash and take the bus home

Just to prove my love I'd tattoo your picture on my chest
Give you all my inheritance and social security checks

Just to show you how much I really care
I'd kneel down on one knee and place 10 karats in the air

Just to have you as a part of my life forever
I'd walk a million miles in cold blue weather

Just to make sure you never walk away
I do roots on you to make you stay

Just so you are mine I'd endure thee unthinkable strife
Put my body on a cross so that our love has everlasting life

I'm crazy for your love and just thought you should know
My life is your existence
My love is your shadow

I'm crazy for your love

Heartbreaking Player

Just as my love for you began to grow
You placed sunlight on a heart made of snow

Just as I leaped high into emotions
You pulled the tricks out of your sleeve

Just when love started to open closed doors
You slammed it on and decided to leave

Just when my feelings got very strong
You ended my perfect dream

Just when I thought you deserved all my heart,
You ripped and tore it apart.

Be careful of players they make molds like clay,
They'll get what they want and leave the next day,

Once they get what they want and accomplish their goal,
You'll be lost and turned out; robbed of your soul

Once your innocence is stolen and you can't believe,
You're left hurt and misused and extremely naïve,

The moral of this story is that love is serious, and players
play games; when you give your all to a player guess who's to blame

It's Our First Night Together

I'm so glad you've come I've been here waiting for you
I'm going to take it nice and slow like real gentleman do

I'm going to dim all the shades and bring out the candle light
I'm going to make sure everything is perfect; going to do everything right

I'm going to look into your eyes and hold your body real tight

This will be a romance to remember—it's our first night

I been dreaming for this day for all so long
I'm going to play the magic tunes; sing your favorite song

You're going to feel most exquisite and extremely divine
Forget your other suitors and become entirely mine

So erase all your worries, place your fears out of sight
I'm going to be in your heart forever. It's our first night.

This letter is to inform you that LET'S BREAK UP.

The Break Up Poem

They say if you truly love something you should let it go,
If it decides to come back you'll forever know.

They say that when love breaks your heart it's something
you truly forbid. You don't die from a broken heart you only wish you did.

Sometimes, when one person goes missing, the whole world seems
depopulated. Human emotions turn to bears and get hibernated.

Trying to forget someone you love is like trying to remember someone you
never knew. It's hard to forget real love when love takes control of you.

The most famous line in a break up is also the most untrue:
I love you BUT I'm not in love with you

The hardest thing to do is watch the one you love go and
love another. It's like a child watching a father abuse his mother

I don't know why they call it heartbreak when the rest of
your body aches too. Symptoms of a breakup can be like that of flu

When someone is unfaithful and it kills you inside, get rid
of that loser and have some pride

When your heart has been broken and you feel you want to
die, become the star that you are and reach high to the sky

There's plenty more players on the bench and fish in the
sea. Let love control you heart, not your destiny

Funny Break Up Quotes

"I really like you but I think you and my cousin are a better match.**"**

"I never liked your mother anyway.**"**

"You're not the one... or the two, or the three!**"**

"There was always something about you I just couldn't put my finger on....I'm glad I didn't!**"**

"Guess what? My ex and I have decided to work things out.**"**

"I want you to always remember me like this... walking out the door!**"**

"I've gotten a job offer out-of-state, how should we split the furniture?**"**

"I'll never forget the day we met... because it's a stain on my existence."

"We're just not on the same page anymore, or even in the same book!"

"I think we want different things; you want to go back to school, and I want to be single."

"Do you know what 1 plus 1 is...? Okay, now subtract 1 from that."

"Living with you is like a prison sentence. Your cooking sucks and I can't wait to get out."

"Don't think of us as over. Think of me as simply OVER you!"

"My doctor says to try new things, so I started with anew language... *Adios amigo!*"

45

Love on the Brain

I've got love on the brain like a train on a track
Like an addict wanting crack
Like Brutality on Black
Like Marines in Iraq
Like Jesus coming back
Carl Lewis on a track

A heart attack
Pounds on fat

Pimp in his hat
Jay Z and a rap

Like a need to ASAP
Like something I lack

I got love on the brain!

Can't Imagine

Can't imagine someone else holding your hand
Claiming a prize meant for only me

Can't imagine your love being shared with another reluctantly

Can't imagine this bed we share empty with space once filled by you

Can't imagine my dreams without your love ever coming true

Can't imagine not seeing your face or all the above

Can't imagine you and someone else making love

Can't imagine a day when we won't be together

That's why I'll play my part to keep you forever

Twenty-Four Hours a Day

I think about what it might be like to marry you
Spend my whole life with you
Have kids and buy a new house for you
Wake up every morning next to you
Make a future map with roads to all of you
Take all your desires and fulfill for you
Commit faithfully and be loyal to you
Write a love song and sing it to you
Rush straight home from work to be with you
Let go of bad habits to please you
Just how much I really need you

Twenty-Four hours a day all I do is think of you

Celebrity Love

Fame loves fame that's the name of the game
Money equals power and egos are to blame

When success pursues love there is much at stake:
Does the suitor really love me?
Will our finances equate?

Hollywood is very famous for the stars it creates
Divorce is very common like the movies it makes

Not many last for long after the knot has been tied
The industry can chew you up and spit out your pride

Whether your gift is to act or your talent is to sing
Insurance is a must when you purchase that ring

Everything has a cost and the price will get paid
When fortune needs trust the heart meets a spade

When loyalty meets lust; heat of passions gets laid
Faithful partners get burned and love starts to fade

Kim Kardashian and Kris didn't make it through
Tom and Kate separated out of the blue

49

Seal and Hiedi couldn't even make it last
Guess they moved to fast

Jennifer and Brad came with so much regret
She should have seen it coming when the Smiths first met

Hillary and Bill are for sure a hard act to follow
Even sexual relations with Monica went over the rainbow

Beyoncé and Jay bring much hope to the game
Although we love Liz Taylor, she gave love a bad name

Ike and Tina went round for round
Glad she had enough and stood her ground

The late Whitney and Bobby a disaster at its best
When they first got together we knew it was a mess

Even the royal in Britain face the same game of fame
Princess Diana and Prince Charles affected the same

How about the man behind the camera for sure he's seen it
all. Spielberg celebrates eleven years with the lovely Capshaw

Let us not forget Iman the Somalian African beauty
Still married happily to Dave Bowie

Will and Jada, a true Hollywood gem
Love continues to last despite rumors to condemn

Last but not least a love that has lasted through quite a
storm. I commend Mr. and Mrs. Ozzy & Sharon Osbourne

50

I Think I'm In Love

I'm starting to get that feeling that simply won't fade away
The thought of you makes me smile each and every day

I'm breaking plans with friends to spend my time with you
Like a 70's greatest hit: You make me feel brand new

I don't know where this is going; but I'm in it for the ride
I usually don't express my feelings; but with you I cannot hide

I think I'm in love with you and my heart can't deny

When You Love Too Fast

Let love take its course without fear or remorse
Be patient while dating let it flow without force

Be subtle when the time comes to say how much you care
Say I love you too fast and the loved one can disappear

Take your time getting to know someone before to them
you give your all. Relationships never workout when you
build your hopes too tall

Lonely hearts sometimes boost about what they think is Mr. Right.
Introduce the family and breakup the next night

Rebounds can be quick giving comfort to love's demise
Its lifespan doesn't stick because the choice is unwise

When someone comes into your life, don't rush love let a
little time pass. Giving titles and such raise the red flags

Make sure you're the only one before you quickly assume
Assuming things irrevocably makes a mule of you

Secretly in Love

To my grave I will take my love for it's the only way
I only hope that you have noticed my love before my dying day

I'll continue to be your friend while I wish we could be more
Every moment we spend together lets me know this for sure

Just when I forget, you call and I'm back under your spell
I think you're also in love with me; but like me won't tell

It's an unfair situation to keep such feelings hidden so deep
within. A painful torture of my love unspoken; while I continue to pretend

Maybe someday I'll confess, and succumb to my pride

For now I'll continue loving moments spent with you while these
feelings for you I hide

I Found Love

I used to dream about love, now I dream for love no more
Crippling voids of loneliness cracked like plate falling
on a floor

Envy of others happiness would make feel so depressed
I'd often pretend to be glad for friends when I couldn't
care less

I had one night stands and acted out foolishly
True romance never came around, not even remotely

I settled for whatever came my way, didn't think I could do
better. Every possible love candidate wrote a
Dear John Letter

Just when I decided I wouldn't give love another try
I found my Stevie Wonder ribbon in the sky

Now I walk a different walk, my heart has been set free
I found someone who accepts all my flaws and
Loves me for me

When It's Over and Done

When all the years of great love suddenly turn into pain
It feels like a ton of tears cry inside a soul, like a hurricane of rain
When the one you care most for decides to walk away
Not even the most precious memory of time together could
make them stay

When you take love for granted, unmindful of the feelings
that you have burned
The shoe gets on the other foot and a lesson is learned

When what you thought would last a lifetime tells you it's
approached the last day
The blame is all on you and the games you decided to play

When you break someone's heart in half, don't expect them
to remain forever true
It's only a matter of time before the table turns and karma gets you

When a good thing comes your way, respect it; mold it best as you can
Concentrating on only your needs gets your heart in the quickest of sand

Unfulfilled hearts premeditate escape; to which turning
back is not always a choice to consider
Reality reaches the depths of your hopes with dismay once
you meet that dreadful river

You only wish you never had that fun
When
Its
Over
Done

Before You Walk Out That Door

Before you say your final goodbye hear me out loud and clear
My life will never be the same without you here

Before you pack your bags I beg you to look deep into my eyes
There's nothing I wouldn't do to make you reconsider
saying goodbye

Although I took something's for granted, I promise from
today to give you all you need
My world without you is a world I can't conceive

Before you say it's too late, think of all the dreams we made together
Success to me means nothing, if you're not in my life forever

Before you close that door let me tell you just five more times
I love you,
I love you,
I love you,
I love you,
I love you!

Baby please be mine

Don't Be So Shocked

You get what you give
You give what you get

The wakeup call always comes when you least expect

It's hard to cry tears when you caused all the pain
Try hard as you may, not a drop you'll attain

What goes around comes back around; that's what people say
The only way to keep a faithful partner, is avoiding lust in your way

A fool always thinks he's wise in his recklessness of disguise
When daylight comes to night, the sun shines on his lies

Not for long will the aching heart stay with its blinded eye
Eventually, enough is enough, and good riddance
is goodbye

You only get away the first time; not the second, or the third

Just because you haven't been seen; doesn't mean you
haven't been heard

Prepare yourselves cheating hearts for sure you will have your day
Take lessons attempters of such, not all shades are gray

This Must Be Hell

What happened to the Angel I fell in love with?
That deep wide smile like a river so deep

Where did that apple in my eye disappear off to?
Those exotic flowers open with perfume to leak

Why do I feel all alone in a crowded room of many faces?
Where is that loving face I know so well?

Did my sins of love get the best of me?
Am I in bad lover's hell?

In The Name Of Love

We can accomplish our goals
Reach the greatest path of success

Move forward from mistakes
Forgive and caress

Share our dreams together
Even when they are not the same

Celebrate life forever
All in the name

Stay in love in any weather
Get pass the moments of pain

I won't leave you ever
Won't take you in vain

Will you marry me?

First Night of Separation

One night without you is one night I can't stand to bear
Empty head prints on the pillow next to me wishing you
was there

Nothing to eat all day, not a hunger in sight
Not a phone call is answered,
No will,
No might

All the sunshine in sky has suddenly disappeared
All the hopes for a future seem clouded with fear

All the things I did wrong, I no longer go near
All the pain I'm feeling now is pain I brought here

I know words are just words and action is the key to love success
If you come back home my love I'll give more than my best

No Riches,
No Success,

No Fantasy,
No Interest,

Could make me happy if it's without the presence of you

Even Though

Even though I told myself I'd be strong and move on with my life
Even though my friends gave me rum and helped me get
through this strife
Even though I stayed out late and danced all night
Even though I believed I would be all right
Even though I didn't want to fight
Even though I got a new poem to write

I won't be happy without you

Not one Day

Not one Hour

Not one minute

Not one second

Not this lifetime

Let's give it one more try

Love

Bob Johnston
137 Island Drive
Hendersonville, TN 37075

NASHVILLE TN 372
24 JUL 2006 PM 3 L

H. Eggers
1705 Crossing Dr
Austin

78741

Suzanne Anderson
Bowling Green OH 43402

Theresa Williams
1800 Bowling Green Road E
Bradner OH 43406

Adriano Shaplin
22 Lafayette Pl.
Burlington VT 05401

Rebecca Wright
C/O NELP
Alton Bay, NH
03810

Letters

Señor
Mario Levrero
Soriano 936 Ap.1
MONTEVIDEO (Uru...

Colección de Poesía   Ocampo 1812 tel 82-21
El Búho Encantado

AIR MAIL
INTERNATIONAL

Sean Hollands
450 London Road
Ditton, Aylesford
...nt ME20 6DA
...land...

POSTAGE PAID

Año jubilar   VIRGEN
de la   CAPILLA

AÑO JUBILAR VIRGEN DE LA CAPILLA
11-JUNIO-61
JAEN

ESPAÑA

CIRCULO...
Casilla ...
BUENOS A...
JAEN   7763

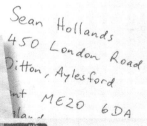

II EXPOSICION DEL
SELLO MISIONAL
BARCELONA, 16-24-MARZO 1958

EXPOSICION SELLO MISIONAL
16-19-MAR.
1958
BARCELONA

EXPOSICION SELLO MIS...
15-19-1-MAR
1958
BARCELONA

80
ESPAÑA

1858 + 1958
CENTENARIO
DE LA APARICION DE
N. S. DE LOURDES

1718

Antonio Fernández Fernández
Apartado 7, AVILES
(Asturias-España)

Love Letters/In Love

Knowing you has been a complete blessing, you don't even understand. I feel like I have won the lottery but I'd like to believe luck had nothing to do with it. The concept of "time" is almost incomprehensible and even still, I want to make the most of our time together.

I am enamored by you and look forward to seeing you next weekend.

-Tiger

Love Letters/In Love

When I told you I would give you anything to make you happy, I wasn't joking. I LOVE YOU more and more as the days go by. Don't EVER go away. I love you Bookie. I truly LOVE you.

                              - Jigger

Love Letters/In Love

I felt it was more appropriate to write my feelings down rather than to buy and borrow that of others in a card. Ever since I met you I haven't been able to stop wondering what it would be like to be more than just a friend. I find myself infatuated with you and wanting my infatuation to evolve into something more serious. It's not that I have had any sleepless nights or constant thoughts. However, one thought was enough to approach the subject and bring my feelings to your attention. The intent of this little note is not to look for an answer or SOLID assumption on your part, but just a mere invitation for us to be closer friends. TIME TELLS ALL!

Sincerely, _____

Love Letters/Falling Out of Love

I'm sorry for screaming at you, it's just that I had enough of your false accusations. As much as I love you and do for you it seems it's never enough! What happened to our love? There was a time you would trust me when I hung out with my friends. Now I can't even talk to them on the phone without you getting upset. I remember when we used to laugh and build dreams in our head for our future. We haven't even made love in two months. I want you to know that you're pushing me away.

Love Letters/Falling Out of Love

This is last time I allow you to stand me up!
You didn't even have the decency to call me until I hour later to say you were cancelling. It seems like you're more into your sports team then you are into me. I want you to know that you're making me feel like I don't mean that much to you anymore. You're gonna need to step your game up or I'm out. This is truly the last time I let you disregard my feelings.

Sincerely,

Love Letters/Falling Out of Love

There's something we need to talk about when you get a chance. I think we may need a little break so we see if this something we really want. Lately I have been feeling like I'm the only one trying to make this work. I really hate it when you walk away from every argument rather than say what you really feel. We are both adults and I refuse to play childish games with you anymore. You think you're never wrong about anything! And that's really starting to get old to me.

Call me, _____

Falling In Love

i love you because you make me look forward to
each day. you're my life, a dream come true. there
are no words to express what i feel for you.
there are no songs as beautiful as the music that
fills my soul when i hear your voice. there are no
roses as lovely as your smile. nothing moves me
like you do. there are no days brighter than the
days i spend talking to you on the phone.
you're my light in the darkness. there could never
be words strong enough to express my love for you.
i love you with all my body, soul, and mind. just
wanted you to know that.

Short

Love Poems

I ♥ You!

Short Love Poem #1

Just when I thought I couldn't dare love another
I find myself head over heels for you, while my heart
rediscovers
I'm calling all the others I was trying to persue
The message that I'm leaving is that I found something
new.

Short Love Poem #2

I've had love in Europe
I've loved in the U.S.A
I have loved quite a many
But never this way
I've had my heart broken
Broke many in my day
I hope there's no more Karma
I hope you stay

Short Love Poem #3

I saw you and you saw me
From that moment on, we were meant to be
The way I feel I can't explain
Maybe it's a supernatural thing

Short Love Poem #4

I remember when our love had sadly ended
I found someone else to love
I forgot about you
I stopped missing you
Now that I see you with him, I miss you
I remember you
I realize I still love you

WASHINGTON MONUMENT AND CHERRY BLOSSOMS, WASHINGTON D. C.

City

Greetings from **NEW YORK CITY**

Paris

A Paris Kind of Love

Let's hold hands and lavish inside our love in the most
romantic city during the spring. Let's walk the steps of the
Eiffel Tower so I can propose surprisingly

Let's venture a long journey to the Louvre to see some
famous classic art. Let's suspend ourselves in the jewel of
French culture with a walk around the Luxembourg Gardens Park

Next the Arc De Triomphe for a view of its iconic structure
Go to a crowded bistro and have someone take a touristy picture

We can't forget the Cathedral of Notre Dame, visits to the
top are completely free and there is never a line. Take the
savings we make and spend it on French wine.

Let's travel to an African cafe in Saint Denis. Share a dish
of Jollif rice and drink Tanzanian tea.

Instead of the traditional box of chocolates, let's do an "All
about Chocolate" spa treatment at the Four Seasons George V hotel.

A chocolate-mint body scrub sweet ecstasy to inhale

Lovers experiencing Paris are in the perfect place to be.

Valentine's Day is every day where souls are set free

80

A New York City Love

The Big Apple has a space large enough for any lovers to play. You can get whatever you want, anytime of the day

Take a walk before dark in Central Park. Eat sushi by the highline window made fresh from Morimoto

Take the A train to 42nd and catch quick Broadway play Go to Juniors for some cheesecake made fresh everyday

Jump on a Staten Island ferry for a glimpse of liberty It's romantic after sunsets and the view is all for free

If the nightlife has your interest; the Meat Packing is the latest for a good show. Start at Standard for some mixed drinks, then Gansevoort where the celebrities glow

Take the L train to Brooklyn to Peter Luger for the best steak NY can make. Be sure to make a reservation; if not you'll surely wait

If true romance you're surely seeking, something suddenly rang a bell, take a Carriage Ride on a white horse and a walk through the Plaza Hotel

If its winter time and you want adventure, there is only one place that I can think; the Rockefeller Center has the iconic skating rink

When you think of NYC skyline no other romantic experience could ever compete. A trip to the top of the Empire State Building is last; but far from being least.

WASHINGTON MONUMENT AND CHERRY BLOSSOMS, WASHINGTON D. C.

A Love in Washington, D.C.

The District of Columbia is built with the perfect romance, and for lovers a great place to glow. From its stunning archives of our history; to amazing captures of the Capitol

Take a walk through the Botanical Gardens you'll see your love also starts to grow. Twenty miles south takes you to Mt. Vernon next to the Cathedral National

Hold hands in Georgetown, or have your picnic beside Gravelly Point. Fill your basket with fresh goods from Eastern Market, and a side from Bens Chili joint

Go to a concert with live bands playing DC's native Go Go beats. Have drinks on the rooftop of Hotel Washington on F and 15th street

Lovers can checkout Oldtown Alexandria, take a cruise with the Potomac view. The sight of the Monuments at night can be romantic like cherry morning dew

If your heart still desires a little more culture, a former exslave can set you free. During a tour of Frederick Douglass mansion it's the capital you can see

Romance is no stranger to the district, Michele and Obama both agree. When you envision true romance in Washington: they put the L in O.V.E

84

A Philadelphia Kind of Love

The City of Brotherly Love is filled with a true romance
and much talent resides within. Not just the home of Will Smith,
and Pattie Labelle, but the great music of Boyz ll Men

Take a newlywed stroll to the south of Broad Street for a
famous grilled cheesesteak. Behind the walls of the famous
Art Museum is the perfect romantic date

Whether you drive in your car or take the path behind the
park, Kelly Drive will you remind you of love and put a
move on your heart

Old City too has charm and so many romantic things to do
Take a stride through Penn's landing for a Spirit dinner cruise
Take a Ghost Tour and get scared for another chance to
hold each other. There's many haunted houses for lovers to discover

Reading Terminal near the Gallery has the best Amish
bread and signature Philly cakes. Chocolate Ben Franklin
candy and best Pretzels man can make

For a super romantic journey in this city where love will
never die, go in January for the mummer's parade, free
Parkway concert in July

For 5 star dining and romantic dinner with extreme
elegance, Le Bec Fin on Walnut Street is quintessential for
foodie celebrants

Before you leave there is a must see in this sports fanatic
city. A homecoming game a Temple were you're sure find
Bill Cosby

Love in the San Francisco Bay

There aren't many more romantic things to do then
trekking the walk across the bridge of the Golden Gate.
Alcatraz Island and Castro can be just as quixotic too, or a
trolley ride after eight

Whether your companion prefers musical comedy or a
thought-provoking play, the American Conservatory
Theater is sure to give you Broadway

Take Salsa lessons at Café Cocomo where you and lover
can dance the night away. Unwind with a glass of wine at
de Young Museum it'll make you feel extremely gay

If you want to make your girl feel warm and fuzzy I know
the perfect place to go. 261 Columbus Avenue,
Booksellers spoken word show

Few experiences are more romantic than sailing pass a
beautiful sunset. Choose a catamaran ride on the Adventure
Cat and let the golden rays make your heart wet

Wine and dine your date with the progressive American
menu and all-California wine list at First Crush.
It'sLocated near the Union Square, with an atmosphere sure to
make her blush

Before you leave San Francisco feel the sand while you
walk hand and hand along the beautiful shore.

Enjoy the views of the bridge and the bay guaranteed to
have you back for more.

Stripped Naked

Discard this tuff prideful layer of skin on my flesh, and then zoom deep beyond the veins to the way of my soul

Look far into the pearly gaze of my pretty eyes with my complete permission

Give me the wake-up call I need

Let the absence of you develop me through the pain

You'll uncover my secrets,

My Flaws,

My weakness,

Then as you see me as you never have before; ill stop pretending to be what I display

I'll correct what I must

I'll regain your trust

I'll be better for us

I'm ready to be stripped

About the Author

Marion D. Ingram is a Renaissance man who is interested in the art and cultural grounds of America, Europe and Africa. He is a well-travelled author and poet. Since 1999, he has produced numerous literary-related special events and has wowed audiences with his cutting-edge brand of poetry at coffeehouses, theaters, and universities across the country and abroad. He hosts "Uncensored Thoughts" through local sponsorship to create an atmosphere for poets to grow through creative writing and works with a nonprofit youth organization (Do The Write Thing of DC) to encourage youth to write and publish collections of poetry. He has also lived abroad in Paris, France where he immersed himself in its culture and held several book signings where he thrilled audiences with his electric readings and performances.

His other published works include:

Uncensored Thoughts, a book of poetry that examines life through hope, love, dedication and exploration.

The State of America, captures American life and culture in photos and essays

Made in the USA
Middletown, DE
23 June 2022

67667193R00051